Introduction

The Importance of Making Smart Decisions

Making smart decisions is essential in our personal and professional lives. Every day, we face decisions that impact our future, our relationships, our careers, and our well-being. The choices we make can have long-lasting consequences, so it's crucial to approach decision-making thoughtfully and intentionally.

Making smart decisions requires careful consideration, analysis, and evaluation of available options. It involves weighing the pros and cons, anticipating the potential outcomes, and understanding the risks and benefits. When we make informed decisions, we can reduce uncertainty, minimize risk, and increase our chances of success.

On the other hand, making poor decisions can have significant negative consequences. It can lead to missed opportunities, damaged relationships, financial losses, and other adverse outcomes. Poor decision-making can also create stress and anxiety, impacting our mental health and well-being.

Moreover, decisions can impact not only ourselves but also those around us. For example, decisions made by business leaders can affect the livelihoods of their employees and the communities they serve. Decisions made by parents can impact the lives of their children. Thus, making smart decisions is not just about personal gain, but it's also about being responsible and mindful of our impact on others.

In summary, making smart decisions is essential to our personal and professional lives. It enables us to achieve our goals, build strong relationships, and create a better future for ourselves and those around us. By taking a thoughtful and intentional approach to decision-making, we can increase our chances of success and minimize the negative consequences of poor decision-making.

Why Decision-Making is Hard

Complexity: Many decisions are complex, and there are often multiple factors to consider, making it challenging to weigh the options and choose the best course of action.

1. Uncertainty: Sometimes, decision-makers lack complete information about the options or potential outcomes, leading to uncertainty and hesitation in making a decision.
2. Emotions: Emotions can play a significant role in decision-making, leading to biases and clouded judgment. For example, fear, anger, or anxiety can cause us to avoid risks or make impulsive decisions.
3. Cognitive Biases: Humans are prone to cognitive biases, which can lead to faulty reasoning and judgment. For example, confirmation bias can cause us to seek out information that confirms our existing beliefs and disregard information that contradicts them.
4. Trade-offs: Many decisions require trade-offs, which can be challenging to balance. For example, choosing between two job offers may require deciding between higher pay and better work-life balance.
5. Pressure: In some situations, decision-makers may face external pressure to make a decision quickly or to choose a particular option, leading to rushed or suboptimal decision-making.
6. Consequences: Decisions can have significant consequences, both positive and negative, making it challenging to take responsibility for the outcome.

In summary, decision-making can be challenging due to several factors, including complexity, uncertainty, emotions, cognitive biases, trade-offs, pressure, and consequences. Being aware of these challenges and taking a thoughtful and intentional approach to decision-making can help overcome these difficulties and make better decisions.

How This Book Can Help You

1. Understanding the decision-making process: The book offers a comprehensive explanation of the decision-making process and how our biases, emotions, and cognitive limitations can influence our choices. By understanding these factors, readers can gain greater insight into their decision-making habits and identify areas for improvement.

2. Identifying decision criteria: One of the key challenges in decision-making is identifying the most important criteria to consider. The book provides a framework for identifying and prioritizing decision criteria based on personal values, objectives, and preferences.

3. Evaluating alternatives: The book offers a systematic approach for evaluating alternative options and assessing their potential outcomes. This can help readers make more informed decisions and minimize the risk of making a poor choice.

4. Managing uncertainty: Many decisions involve a degree of uncertainty, which can make the decision-making process more challenging. The book provides strategies for managing uncertainty and making decisions in situations where the outcome is uncertain.

5. Dealing with difficult decisions: Making tough decisions can be emotionally draining and stressful. The book offers guidance on how to approach difficult decisions, including how to manage emotions, seek advice, and weigh the pros and cons of different options.

6. Applying decision-making skills to real-world situations: The book includes numerous case studies and examples of decision-making in various contexts, such as business, health care, and personal relationships. This helps readers apply the decision-making skills they learn to real-world situations and understand how to make better decisions in their own lives.

In summary, "Smart Choices: How to Make the Best Decision at All Times, Even When It's Difficult" offers practical guidance and strategies for making effective decisions in all aspects of life. Whether you're faced with a difficult personal choice or a complex business decision, this book can help you make more informed, confident decisions that lead to better outcomes.

Chapter 1

Understanding the Decision-Making Process

Understanding the decision-making process is a critical step towards making better choices. The process of decision-making involves several steps, and each step can be influenced by different factors such as emotions, biases, personal values, and cognitive limitations. Here are the key steps involved in the decision-making process:

1. Identify the Decision: The first step is to identify the decision that needs to be made. This may involve identifying a problem that needs to be solved or a goal that needs to be achieved.

2. Gather Information: Once the decision has been identified, the next step is to gather information. This may involve researching the available options, seeking advice from experts, and gathering data to help inform the decision.

3. Identify Criteria: After gathering information, it's important to identify the criteria that will be used to evaluate the available options. Criteria may include factors such as cost, quality, feasibility, and impact on stakeholders.

4. Evaluate Alternatives: With the criteria in mind, the next step is to evaluate the available alternatives. This may involve weighing the pros and cons of each option, considering the potential risks and benefits, and assessing how well each option meets the established criteria.

5. Make a Decision: Based on the evaluation of the alternatives, a decision can be made. This decision may involve selecting the best option, deciding to pursue multiple options, or deciding not to pursue any of the available options.

6. Take Action: Once a decision has been made, it's important to take action to implement the decision. This may involve developing an action plan, assigning responsibilities, and monitoring progress to ensure that the decision is successfully implemented.

7. Evaluate the Decision: After the decision has been implemented, it's important to evaluate its effectiveness. This may involve assessing whether the decision achieved the desired outcome, identifying areas for improvement, and making any necessary adjustments.

By understanding the decision-making process, individuals can identify the steps where they may be prone to making errors or biased judgments, and take steps to mitigate these risks. Additionally, understanding the decision-making process can help individuals make more informed, rational decisions that are aligned with their goals and values.

The Role of Intuition vs. Logic in Decision-Making

The role of intuition versus logic in decision-making is an ongoing debate. Intuition is often associated with a gut feeling or a hunch, while logic is associated with rational thinking and analysis. Both intuition and logic have their strengths and weaknesses, and their role in decision-making may depend on the specific situation and individual preferences.

Intuition can be beneficial in decision-making in several ways. For example, intuition can help individuals identify patterns or connections that may not be immediately apparent through logical analysis. Intuition can also help individuals make quick decisions in situations where time is limited, or where there is insufficient information to make a rational decision. Additionally, intuition can be helpful in situations where emotions are involved, as it can help individuals identify their feelings and react accordingly.

However, intuition also has its limitations. Intuition can be influenced by biases, emotions, and personal experiences, which may lead to inaccurate or irrational decisions. Additionally, relying too heavily on intuition can lead to impulsive decision-making, which may not always be in an individual's best interest.

Logic, on the other hand, is a more systematic approach to decision-making. Logical thinking involves breaking down complex problems into smaller components, evaluating the evidence, and weighing the pros and cons of different options. Logical thinking can be helpful in situations where there is a need for an objective analysis of the available options, and where there is a need to make decisions based on facts and evidence.

However, logical thinking also has its limitations. It can be time-consuming and may not always be feasible in situations where there is a need for quick decision-making. Additionally, logical thinking may not always take into account the emotional or subjective factors that can influence decision-making.

In conclusion, both intuition and logic can play a role in decision-making, and their importance may depend on the specific situation and individual preferences. It's important to be aware of the strengths and weaknesses of each approach and to use a combination of intuition and logic to make effective decisions. By balancing intuition and logic, individuals can make more informed, rational decisions that are aligned with their goals and values.

Types of Decisions You'll Encounter

In life, we encounter different types of decisions that require different levels of analysis, evaluation, and judgment. Here are some common types of decisions that individuals encounter:

1. Routine Decisions: These are everyday decisions that do not require a lot of thought or analysis, such as what to wear, what to eat, or what route to take to work.

2. Strategic Decisions: These are decisions that have a significant impact on an individual or an organization, such as entering a new market, launching a new product, or making a major investment. Strategic decisions typically involve extensive analysis, evaluation, and risk assessment.

3. Operational Decisions: These are decisions that are made on a daily basis to ensure the smooth running of an organization or business, such as scheduling employees, ordering supplies, or managing inventory.

4. Tactical Decisions: These are decisions that are made in response to specific situations or challenges, such as changing market conditions, unexpected events, or unforeseen problems. Tactical decisions are typically made quickly, and they may involve adjusting strategies, processes, or resources to address the situation at hand.

5. Personal Decisions: These are decisions that are made in an individual's personal life, such as where to live, whom to marry, or what career path to pursue. Personal decisions are often influenced by an individual's values, beliefs, and emotions , and they can have a significant impact on an individual's happiness and well-being.

6. Group Decisions: These are decisions that are made collectively by a group of individuals, such as a team, a board of directors, or a community organization. Group decisions can be challenging as they require individuals to work together to achieve a common goal while balancing different perspectives, opinions, and interests.

In conclusion, individuals encounter different types of decisions in their personal and professional lives, and each type of decision requires a different level of analysis, evaluation, and judgment. By understanding the types of decisions they encounter and the factors that influence their decision-making, individuals can make more informed, effective decisions that are aligned with their goals and values.

Common Decision-Making Pitfalls to Avoid

While decision-making is an essential skill, it's important to be aware of common pitfalls that can lead to poor decision-making. Here are some common decision-making pitfalls to avoid:

1. Confirmation Bias: This occurs when individuals seek out information that confirms their preexisting beliefs, while ignoring information that contradicts those beliefs. To avoid confirmation bias, individuals should actively seek out and consider information that challenges their assumptions and beliefs.

2. Overconfidence: This occurs when individuals overestimate their abilities or the likelihood of a particular outcome. To avoid overconfidence, individuals should consider a range of possible outcomes and the likelihood of each one occurring.

3. Groupthink: This occurs when a group of individuals make decisions without considering alternative viewpoints or challenging the group's consensus. To avoid groupthink, individuals should encourage dissenting opinions and consider a range of perspectives.

4. Anchoring Bias: This occurs when individuals rely too heavily on the first piece of information they encounter, even if that information is inaccurate or incomplete. To avoid anchoring bias, individuals should consider a range of information and avoid making snap judgments based on limited information.

5. Sunk Cost Fallacy: This occurs when individuals continue to invest time, money, or resources into a project or decision, even if the costs outweigh the benefits. To avoid sunk cost fallacy, individuals should consider the current costs and benefits of a decision, rather than focusing on past investments.

6. Emotion-based Decision Making: This occurs when individuals make decisions based on their emotions rather than objective analysis. To avoid emotion-based decision-making, individuals should take time to consider their emotions and separate them from the decision-making process.

7. Analysis Paralysis: This occurs when individuals become overwhelmed by the amount of information available and struggle to make a decision. To avoid analysis paralysis, individuals should focus on the most important information and make a decision based on that information.

In conclusion, by being aware of common decision-making pitfalls, individuals can avoid making poor decisions and make more informed, effective decisions that are aligned with their goals and values.

Chapter 2

Identifying Your Values and Priorities

Identifying your values and priorities is an essential step in making effective decisions that align with your goals and beliefs. Here are some steps you can take to identify your values and priorities:

1. Reflect on your past decisions: Think about the decisions you've made in the past and what motivated you to make those decisions. Consider the outcomes of those decisions and whether they were aligned with your goals and values.

2. Identify your core values: Consider the values that are most important to you, such as honesty, integrity, kindness, or compassion. These values can guide your decision-making and help you prioritize what is most important to you.

3. Consider your long-term goals: Think about your long-term goals, such as your career aspirations, personal relationships, or financial objectives. These goals can help you prioritize your decisions and determine what actions you need to take to achieve them.

4. Determine your priorities: Consider the areas of your life that are most important to you, such as family, friends, career, or personal growth. These priorities can help you make decisions that align with your values and goals.

5. Evaluate trade-offs: Sometimes, you may need to make a decision that requires you to prioritize one value or goal over another. In these situations, consider the trade-offs and determine which decision is most aligned with your values and priorities.

6. Seek feedback: Seek feedback from others who share your values and priorities. They can provide a different perspective and help you make more informed decisions.

By identifying your values and priorities, you can make more informed, effective decisions that are aligned with your goals and beliefs. Additionally, having a clear understanding of your values and priorities can help you navigate difficult decisions and make choices that bring you greater satisfaction and fulfillment.

Prioritizing Your Goals and Objectives

Prioritizing your goals and objectives is a crucial step in making effective decisions that are aligned with your long-term vision. Here are some steps you can take to prioritize your goals and objectives:

1. Create a list of goals and objectives: Start by making a list of your goals and objectives. Consider your short-term and long-term goals, such as career advancement, personal growth, financial stability, or relationships.

2. Evaluate each goal or objective: Evaluate each goal or objective based on its importance and urgency. Consider the impact it will have on your life and how it aligns with your values and priorities.

3. Assign a priority level: Once you have evaluated each goal or objective, assign a priority level to each one. Use a numbering system, such as 1 for the most important, 2 for moderately important, and 3 for the least important.

4. Consider trade-offs: Sometimes, you may need to prioritize one goal or objective over another. Consider the trade-offs and determine which goal is most aligned with your values and priorities.

5. Review and update your priorities regularly: Your priorities may change over time, so it's important to review and update your list regularly. Set aside time to evaluate your goals and objectives periodically and make adjustments as needed.

6. Focus on the most important goals: Once you have identified your most important goals and objectives, focus on them first. This can help you make progress towards achieving your long-term vision and increase your sense of accomplishment and satisfaction.

By prioritizing your goals and objectives, you can make more informed, effective decisions that are aligned with your long-term vision. Additionally, having a clear understanding of your priorities can help you manage your time and resources more effectively, increase your productivity, and reduce stress and overwhelm.

Aligning Your Decisions with Your Values

Aligning your decisions with your values is a critical component of making effective and satisfying choices. When your decisions align with your values, you are more likely to feel fulfilled, confident, and satisfied with the outcomes. Here are some steps you can take to align your decisions with your values:

1. Identify your core values: Begin by identifying your core values. These are the principles and beliefs that are most important to you and guide your behavior and decision-making. Your core values may include things like honesty, integrity, compassion, or creativity.

2. Determine your priorities: Once you have identified your core values, determine your priorities. Think about the areas of your life that are most important to you, such as family, relationships, career, or personal growth.

3. Evaluate your options: When faced with a decision, evaluate your options based on how well they align with your values and priorities. Consider the potential outcomes of each option and how they may impact your life in the short-term and long-term.

4. Consider the consequences: Think about the potential consequences of your decisions. How will your decision impact your relationships, your goals, and your values? Consider both the positive and negative consequences of each option.

5. Seek feedback: Seek feedback from people who share your values and priorities. They can offer a different perspective and help you make a more informed decision that aligns with your values.

6. Take action: Once you have evaluated your options and determined which decision aligns best with your values and priorities, take action. Trust yourself and have confidence in your decision, knowing that it is in alignment with your values and goals.

By aligning your decisions with your values, you can make more informed and fulfilling choices that support your long-term vision and bring you greater satisfaction and happiness. Additionally, when you prioritize your values and beliefs, you build a stronger sense of self-awareness and integrity, which can help you make more confident and authentic decisions in all areas of your life.

Dealing with Conflicting Priorities

Dealing with conflicting priorities can be a challenging aspect of decision-making. It can be difficult to prioritize one objective over another when they are both important and have competing demands. Here are some steps you can take to deal with conflicting priorities:

1. Identify the conflicting priorities: Begin by identifying the conflicting priorities. Determine which objectives are in conflict and the specific reasons why they are in conflict.

2. Consider the consequences: Think about the potential consequences of each decision. Consider both the short-term and long-term implications of each option. This can help you weigh the costs and benefits of each choice.

3. Determine your values: Determine your values and priorities. Consider how each option aligns with your values and which option will support your overall vision and goals.

4. Seek feedback: Seek feedback from trusted advisors or mentors who share your values and priorities. They can offer a different perspective and help you evaluate your options more objectively.

5. Evaluate trade-offs: Evaluate the trade-offs between the conflicting priorities. Determine which objective is most critical and which can be postponed or delegated to a later time.

6. Consider creative solutions: Consider creative solutions that may allow you to meet both objectives. Look for ways to compromise or find a win-win solution that satisfies both priorities.
7. Make a decision: Once you have evaluated your options, make a decision. Trust yourself and have confidence in your decision, knowing that it is the best choice given the conflicting priorities.

By dealing with conflicting priorities, you can make more informed and fulfilling choices that support your long-term vision and bring you greater satisfaction and happiness. Additionally, when you prioritize your values and beliefs, you build a stronger sense of self-awareness and integrity, which can help you make more confident and authentic decisions in all areas of your life.

Chapter 3

Gathering Information and Analyzing Options

Researching Your Options

Researching your options is an important step in making informed and effective decisions. It involves gathering information and data about the various options available to you so that you can make an informed choice. Here are some steps you can take to research your options:

1. Identify the available options: Begin by identifying all the options available to you. Consider the various alternatives, including those that may be less obvious or unconventional.

2. Gather information: Once you have identified your options, gather information about each one. This may involve conducting research, reading reviews or testimonials, consulting with experts, or seeking advice from friends and family.

3. Evaluate the pros and cons: Evaluate the pros and cons of each option. Consider the advantages and disadvantages of each alternative, and how they align with your values and priorities.
4. Consider the costs: Consider the costs of each option. This includes both the monetary costs as well as the time and effort required to pursue each alternative.

5. Evaluate the potential outcomes: Evaluate the potential outcomes of each option. Consider the short-term and long-term implications of each choice, and how they align with your goals and objectives.
6. Seek feedback: Seek feedback from others who have experience with the options you are considering. This can provide valuable insights and perspectives that can help you make a more informed decision.

7. Make a decision: Once you have gathered and evaluated all the information, make a decision. Trust yourself and have confidence in your

decision, knowing that it is based on careful research and evaluation of all available options.

By researching your options, you can make more informed and satisfying decisions that support your long-term vision and bring you greater satisfaction and happiness. Additionally, when you prioritize your values and beliefs and gather information to support your decision-making, you build a stronger sense of self-awareness and integrity, which can help you make more confident and authentic decisions in all areas of your life.

Evaluating the Pros and Cons

Evaluating the pros and cons of a decision is a critical step in making informed and effective choices. It involves weighing the advantages and disadvantages of each option and considering how they align with your values, goals, and priorities. Here are some steps you can take to evaluate the pros and cons of a decision:

1. Identify the pros and cons: Begin by identifying the pros and cons of each option. List out all the advantages and disadvantages of each alternative.

2. Evaluate the importance of each factor: Evaluate the importance of each factor. Consider which factors are most critical to you and which ones are less important. This can help you prioritize the pros and cons and weigh their relative importance.

3. Consider the short-term and long-term implications: Consider the short-term and long-term implications of each factor. Some pros and cons may have immediate consequences, while others may have long-term implications that are not immediately apparent.

4. Consider the potential risks and rewards: Consider the potential risks and rewards of each option. Evaluate the potential benefits and drawbacks of each alternative and weigh them against each other.

5. Evaluate the trade-offs: Evaluate the trade-offs between the pros and cons. Consider which factors are most critical and which ones you may be willing to compromise on.

6. Seek feedback: Seek feedback from others who have experience with the options you are considering. This can provide valuable insights and perspectives that can help you evaluate the pros and cons more objectively.

7. Make a decision: Once you have evaluated the pros and cons of each option, make a decision. Trust yourself and have confidence in your decision, knowing that it is based on careful evaluation of all available options.

By evaluating the pros and cons of a decision, you can make more informed and fulfilling choices that support your long-term vision and bring you greater satisfaction and happiness. Additionally, when you prioritize your values and beliefs and evaluate the pros and cons to support your decision-making, you build a stronger sense of self-awareness and integrity, which can help you make more confident and authentic decisions in all areas of your life.

Using Decision-Making Tools and Techniques

Using decision-making tools and techniques can help you make more informed and effective decisions. There are several different tools and techniques that you can use, depending on the complexity and importance of the decision. Here are some commonly used decision-making tools and techniques:

1. Decision matrix: A decision matrix is a tool that helps you evaluate the pros and cons of different options based on specific criteria. It involves listing the criteria and weighing them according to their importance. Each option is then evaluated against each criterion and given a score, which is used to determine the best option.

2. Cost-benefit analysis: A cost-benefit analysis involves evaluating the costs and benefits of each option. The costs may include monetary costs, time, effort, and other resources. The benefits may include increased revenue, improved productivity, and other positive outcomes. The analysis helps you determine which option provides the greatest benefit relative to its cost.

3. SWOT analysis: A SWOT analysis is a tool that helps you evaluate the strengths, weaknesses, opportunities, and threats of each option. It helps you identify the internal and external factors that may impact each option and evaluate them against each other.

4. Pareto analysis: A Pareto analysis involves identifying the most significant factors that contribute to a decision and focusing on those factors. The analysis helps you prioritize your efforts and resources and focus on the factors that have the greatest impact.

5. Decision trees: A decision tree is a tool that helps you visualize the various options and potential outcomes of a decision. It involves creating a diagram that shows the various options and the consequences of each option. The decision tree helps you evaluate the potential outcomes and choose the best option.

6. Scenario planning: Scenario planning involves creating different scenarios based on different assumptions and evaluating the potential outcomes of

each scenario. The technique helps you prepare for different eventualities and choose the best option based on the most likely scenario.

By using decision-making tools and techniques, you can make more informed and effective decisions that align with your values, goals, and priorities. These tools and techniques help you evaluate the pros and cons of each option, prioritize your efforts and resources, and make the best choice based on the most likely outcomes.

Dealing with Analysis Paralysis

Analysis paralysis is a state of overthinking or over-analyzing a decision to the point where it becomes difficult or impossible to make a choice. It can be caused by fear of making the wrong decision, uncertainty about the outcomes of each option, or a lack of confidence in one's ability to make the right choice. Here are some ways to deal with analysis paralysis:

1. Set a deadline: Set a deadline for making a decision. This helps create a sense of urgency and gives you a clear timeframe for making a choice. If you are still uncertain by the deadline, choose the option that aligns best with your values and priorities.

2. Limit your options: Limit the number of options you are considering. Having too many options can be overwhelming and make it more difficult to make a choice. Choose a few options that align with your values and priorities and evaluate them carefully.

3. Focus on the most critical factors: Focus on the most critical factors when making a decision. Identify the factors that are most important to you and evaluate the options based on those factors. This helps you prioritize your efforts and resources and focus on the most important factors.

4. Seek advice: Seek advice from someone you trust or who has experience with the decision you are facing. This can provide valuable insights and perspectives that can help you evaluate the options more objectively.

5. Use decision-making tools and techniques: Use decision-making tools and techniques to evaluate the options more objectively. This helps you weigh the pros and cons of each option and choose the best one based on your priorities and values.

6. Take action: Take action even if you are uncertain. It is better to make a decision and take action than to remain paralyzed by indecision. Remember that you can always make adjustments as you go along and learn from your experiences.

By dealing with analysis paralysis, you can make more confident and fulfilling decisions that support your long-term vision and bring you greater satisfaction and happiness. Additionally, by prioritizing your values and beliefs and using decision-making tools and techniques, you build a stronger sense of self-awareness and integrity, which can help you make more confident and authentic decisions in all areas of your life.

Chapter 4

Making the Best Decision in Difficult Situations

Dealing with Uncertainty and Risk

Dealing with uncertainty and risk is an essential part of decision-making. Uncertainty arises when the outcomes of the options are unclear, and risk occurs when the outcomes involve potential negative consequences. Here are some ways to deal with uncertainty and risk:

1. Gather information: The more information you have about the options and potential outcomes, the better equipped you are to make a decision. Research and analyze the options thoroughly, and seek out expert opinions or advice if necessary.

2. Evaluate the risks: Identify the potential risks involved with each option, and evaluate them based on their likelihood and potential impact. This helps you weigh the risks against the potential benefits and make a more informed decision.

3. Consider multiple scenarios: Consider multiple scenarios of what could happen under each option. This helps you anticipate potential outcomes and prepare for them in advance.

4. Consider your risk tolerance: Consider your personal risk tolerance when making a decision. Some people are more risk-averse than others, and this can impact the decision-making process. If you are risk-averse, you may

want to choose the option with the least amount of risk, even if it has a lower potential payoff.

5. Consider the long-term consequences: Consider the long-term consequences of each option, not just the short-term benefits or risks. This helps you make a more strategic decision that aligns with your long-term goals and values.

6. Take action: Once you have evaluated the risks and uncertainties, take action. Remember that no decision is entirely risk-free, and you can always adjust your approach based on new information or experiences.

By dealing with uncertainty and risk, you can make more informed and strategic decisions that support your long-term vision and bring you greater satisfaction and happiness. Additionally, by considering your risk tolerance and evaluating the long-term consequences, you build a stronger sense of self-awareness and integrity, which can help you make more confident and authentic decisions in all areas of your life.

Managing Emotions and Stress

Emotions and stress can significantly impact our decision-making abilities. When we are stressed or overwhelmed, our ability to make sound judgments and think critically can be impaired. Therefore, it is crucial to manage our emotions and stress levels to make the best decisions possible. Here are some strategies for managing emotions and stress during the decision-making process:

1. Take a break: If you're feeling overwhelmed or stressed, take a break from the decision-making process. Engage in an activity that relaxes you, such as yoga or meditation, to reduce your stress levels and clear your mind.
2. Identify your emotions: Identify your emotions and acknowledge them. Naming your emotions can help you understand them better and avoid making rash decisions based on them.

3. Practice mindfulness: Practicing mindfulness techniques, such as deep breathing, can help you stay calm and centered during the decision-making process.

4. Seek support: Talk to a trusted friend or family member about your decision, or seek the advice of a professional. Having a supportive network can help you manage your emotions and gain perspective.

5. Reframe negative thoughts: If you find yourself caught up in negative self-talk, reframe your thoughts. Replace negative thoughts with positive, empowering ones to boost your confidence and improve your decision-making abilities.

6. Prioritize self-care: Prioritize self-care activities, such as exercise, healthy eating, and getting enough sleep.

Overcoming Biases and Assumptions

Making decisions is an essential part of life, and it's natural for individuals to rely on their personal biases and assumptions while making decisions. However, biases and assumptions can lead to faulty decision-making, which can have negative consequences. Therefore, it's essential to learn how to overcome biases and assumptions in decision-making. Here are some strategies that can help:

1. Recognize your biases: The first step in overcoming biases is to recognize them. Self-awareness is crucial in identifying personal biases that may affect decision-making. It's important to question assumptions, thoughts, and beliefs and consider how they may influence your decisions.

2. Seek out diverse perspectives: It's easy to become entrenched in our own opinions, but seeking out diverse perspectives can help broaden our understanding and reduce biases. When making decisions, seek out individuals with different backgrounds, perspectives, and experiences to provide input.

3. Consider alternative options: Biases and assumptions can often lead to a narrow focus on a single option. It's important to consider alternative options and weigh the pros and cons of each. This can help reduce the impact of biases and increase the chances of making a well-informed decision.

4. Evaluate evidence objectively: When making decisions, it's essential to evaluate evidence objectively. Consider the quality and reliability of the evidence and avoid letting personal biases and assumptions influence the interpretation of the data.

5. Take time to reflect: Rushed decisions can often be influenced by biases and assumptions. Taking time to reflect on a decision and considering the potential consequences can help reduce biases and lead to more informed decision-making.

In conclusion, biases and assumptions can have a significant impact on decision-making. Recognizing personal biases, seeking out diverse perspectives, considering alternative options, evaluating evidence objectively, and taking time to reflect can help overcome biases and lead to more informed decision-making.

Decision-Making in High-Pressure Environments

Making decisions in high-pressure environments can be challenging as the stakes are often high, and the consequences of poor decision-making can be severe. However, with the right mindset and tools, it is possible to make informed decisions in high-pressure situations. Here are some strategies that can help:

1. Stay calm and focused: High-pressure environments can be stressful, and stress can impair judgment and decision-making abilities. It is essential to stay calm and focused, which can help maintain clarity and increase the chances of making informed decisions.

2. Identify the key decision factors: In high-pressure situations, it's easy to become overwhelmed and lose sight of the key decision factors. Identifying the critical factors can help focus decision-making efforts and ensure that the most important aspects are considered.

3. Gather all relevant information: In high-pressure environments, decisions are often made quickly, which can lead to incomplete or inaccurate information. Taking the time to gather all relevant information can help ensure that decisions are based on the best available data.

4. Consider the short and long-term consequences: High-pressure decisions often have both short and long-term consequences. It's important to consider both to ensure that decisions are sustainable and will not cause further problems down the line.

5. Consult with experts: In high-pressure environments, decisions can have significant consequences. It's important to seek out experts in the relevant fields to provide input and advice, which can help ensure that decisions are well-informed and have the best chance of success.

6. Have contingency plans: High-pressure environments can be unpredictable, and decisions may not always have the desired outcome. Having contingency plans in place can help mitigate the risk of failure and provide alternative options if necessary.

In conclusion, making decisions in high-pressure environments can be challenging, but with the right mindset and tools, it is possible to make informed decisions. Staying calm and focused, identifying key decision factors, gathering relevant information, considering short and long-term consequences, consulting with experts, and having contingency plans can help increase the chances of making successful decisions in high-pressure situations.

Chapter 5

Making Group Decisions

The Dynamics of Group Decision-Making

Group decision-making refers to the process of making decisions by a group of individuals working together towards a common goal. While group decision-making can be beneficial in many ways, it can also be complex and challenging. Understanding the dynamics of group decision-making can help individuals participate more effectively in group decision-making processes. Here are some key dynamics to consider:

1. Group composition: The composition of the group can significantly affect group decision-making. It is essential to have a diverse group of individuals with different backgrounds, experiences, and perspectives. This can help ensure that a range of options and ideas are considered, leading to better decision-making outcomes.

2. Communication: Effective communication is crucial in group decision-making. Members of the group must be able to communicate effectively with each other, share their thoughts and ideas, and provide feedback constructively. Communication should be open and honest to ensure that all members feel heard and respected.

3. Group norms: Group norms refer to the unwritten rules that govern behavior within a group. These norms can significantly influence group decision-making. It is important to establish clear and positive norms that encourage open communication, constructive feedback, and a willingness to consider alternative perspectives.

4. Leadership: Leadership is essential in group decision-making. A leader can help guide the discussion, ensure that all members are included, and facilitate the decision-making process. Effective leadership can help ensure that the group stays focused on the task at hand and that the decision-making process remains productive.

5. Conflict resolution: Conflicts are inevitable in group decision-making, and it is essential to have a process in place to resolve conflicts constructively. Conflicts should be viewed as an opportunity to explore different perspectives and find a compromise that benefits the group as a whole.

6. Decision-making process: Finally, the decision-making process itself is essential. The process should be well-structured, transparent, and inclusive. It should provide opportunities for all members to contribute their ideas and opinions, and the final decision should be based on a thorough analysis of all available options.

In conclusion, understanding the dynamics of group decision-making can help individuals participate more effectively in group decision-making processes. Group composition, communication, group norms, leadership, conflict resolution, and the decision-making process are all essential elements to consider when making decisions as a group. By considering these dynamics, groups can make more informed and effective decisions that benefit everyone involved.

Techniques for Facilitating Group Decisions

Facilitating group decisions can be a complex and challenging task, but there are several techniques that can help make the process more effective. Here are some techniques for facilitating group decisions:

1. Brainstorming: Brainstorming is a technique used to generate a large number of ideas from group members. In this technique, group members are encouraged to express any idea that comes to mind without any criticism or evaluation. This helps generate a wide range of ideas that can then be evaluated and narrowed down to the most suitable option.

2. Nominal group technique: This technique is used to prioritize ideas generated through brainstorming. Group members are asked to rank the ideas individually, and the scores are then aggregated to identify the most favored option.

3. Delphi technique: This technique involves a series of surveys where the group members anonymously provide their input on a particular issue. The results are then analyzed, and feedback is given to the group members. This technique is helpful when the group members have diverse backgrounds and opinions.

4. SWOT analysis: SWOT (Strengths, Weaknesses, Opportunities, and Threats) analysis is a technique that helps identify the internal strengths and weaknesses of a group or organization, as well as external opportunities and threats. This technique helps the group understand the context of the decision and develop an informed perspective.

5. Multi-voting: Multi-voting is a technique used to identify the most popular option from a set of alternatives. Group members are given a certain number of votes that they can use to vote for their preferred option. The option with the most votes is then selected as the final decision.

6. Consensus-building: Consensus-building is a technique used to reach a decision that is agreeable to all group members. In this technique, group members are encouraged to express their concerns and ideas, and the group works together to find a solution that everyone can support.

In conclusion, facilitating group decisions can be challenging, but there are several techniques that can help make the process more effective. Brainstorming, nominal group technique, Delphi technique, SWOT analysis, multi-voting, and consensus-building are some of the techniques that can be used to facilitate group decisions. It is important to select the appropriate technique for the situation and to ensure that all group members are engaged and included in the decision-making process.

Resolving Conflict and Achieving Consensus

Resolving conflicts and achieving consensus is essential for effective group decision-making. Conflict can arise when group members have different perspectives, ideas, or preferences, and can lead to tension and disagreement within the group. However, conflict can also be an opportunity for the group to explore different perspectives and find a compromise that benefits everyone involved. Here are some techniques for resolving conflict and achieving consensus:

1. Active listening: Active listening is essential for resolving conflicts and achieving consensus. It involves paying attention to what the other person is saying, asking questions to clarify their perspective, and acknowledging their feelings and concerns. By listening actively, group members can gain a better understanding of each other's perspectives and work towards a solution that meets everyone's needs.

2. Finding common ground: When conflicts arise, it is important to find common ground between group members. This involves identifying shared interests, goals, and values and working towards a solution that aligns with them. By focusing on shared interests, the group can find a solution that benefits everyone involved.

3. Compromise: Compromise involves finding a solution that meets the needs of all group members, even if it is not the ideal solution for everyone. Compromise requires a willingness to give and take, and may involve finding a solution that is less than perfect but is acceptable to everyone involved.

4. Mediation: Mediation involves bringing in a neutral third party to help resolve conflicts and achieve consensus. The mediator helps facilitate the discussion, ensure that everyone is heard, and guide the group towards a solution that everyone can support.

5. Consensus-building: Consensus-building involves working towards a decision that everyone in the group can support. This technique requires active listening, finding common ground, and compromise. The goal is to find a solution that is acceptable to everyone involved.

In conclusion, resolving conflicts and achieving consensus is essential for effective group decision-making. Active listening, finding common ground, compromise, mediation, and consensus-building are some techniques that can be used to resolve conflicts and achieve consensus. It is important to approach conflicts as an opportunity for learning and growth, and to work towards a solution that meets the needs of all group members.

The Role of Leadership in Group Decision-Making

Leadership plays a crucial role in group decision-making. A good leader is responsible for guiding the group towards a decision that is effective, efficient, and meets the needs of all group members. Here are some of the ways in which leadership can influence group decision-making:

1. Setting the tone: The leader sets the tone for the group and establishes the norms and expectations for the decision-making process. A good leader encourages open communication, active listening, and constructive feedback, which helps create an environment where everyone feels comfortable expressing their ideas and opinions.

2. Facilitating the process: The leader is responsible for facilitating the decision-making process and ensuring that everyone has the opportunity to contribute. This involves guiding the group through each stage of the decision-making process, providing structure and direction, and ensuring that the group stays on track.

3. Encouraging diversity of thought: A good leader encourages diversity of thought and values the different perspectives and experiences that each group member brings to the table. By valuing diversity, the leader can help the group explore different ideas and perspectives, which can lead to more innovative and effective solutions.

4. Managing conflicts: The leader is responsible for managing conflicts and ensuring that the group stays focused on the task at hand. This involves addressing conflicts as they arise, finding common ground between group members, and working towards a solution that everyone can support.

5. Making the final decision: Ultimately, the leader is responsible for making the final decision. However, a good leader will ensure that the decision is based on the input and feedback of all group members, and that everyone understands and supports the decision.

In conclusion, the role of leadership in group decision-making is essential. A good leader sets the tone for the group, facilitates the decision-making process, encourages diversity of thought, manages conflicts, and makes the final decision based on the input and feedback of all group members. By taking on these responsibilities, a good leader can help the group make more effective, efficient, and inclusive decisions.

Chapter 6

Decision-Making in Personal Relationships

The Intersection of Emotion and Logic in Personal Relationships

The intersection of emotion and logic in personal relationships plays a crucial role in decision-making processes. While logic helps us weigh the pros and cons of a situation, emotions provide us with the motivation to take action. In personal relationships, these two factors are often at odds with each other, making it challenging to make decisions that align with our goals and desires.

One example of the intersection of emotion and logic in personal relationships is when deciding whether to stay in or leave a romantic relationship. Logic tells us to weigh the pros and cons of the relationship objectively, taking into account factors such as compatibility, communication, and shared values. On the other hand, emotions such as love, attachment, and fear of being alone can cloud our judgment and influence our decision-making process.

Another example of the intersection of emotion and logic is in family relationships. Deciding whether to forgive a family member who has wronged us can be difficult, as emotions such as anger and hurt can cloud our judgment. Logic can help us to see the situation objectively and weigh the pros and cons of forgiveness, taking into account factors such as the impact on the relationship, our own mental health, and the potential for reconciliation.

In any personal relationship, the intersection of emotion and logic requires us to balance our feelings with rational thought. While emotions can provide us with valuable insights into our own needs and desires, logic can help us to make decisions that align with our long-term goals and values. By finding a balance between these two factors, we can make decisions that promote healthy and fulfilling relationships.

Making Decisions as a Couple or Family

Making decisions as a couple or family is a complex process that requires effective communication, compromise, and a willingness to consider the needs and desires of all members involved. Whether it's deciding on a major purchase, where to go on vacation, or how to handle a difficult situation, the decision-making process can be challenging, especially when multiple people are involved.

One important aspect of making decisions as a couple or family is to establish clear communication channels. Each member should have the opportunity to express their thoughts and feelings, and everyone should be willing to listen and understand each other's perspectives. It's essential to avoid interrupting or dismissing one another, as this can lead to hurt feelings and misunderstandings.

Another critical factor in making decisions as a couple or family is to identify shared goals and values. When making a decision, it's important to consider how it aligns with the family's long-term goals and values. For example, if one member wants to buy a new car, but the family's goal is to save for a down payment on a home, the decision may need to be re-evaluated in light of the family's priorities.

Compromise is also crucial when making decisions as a couple or family. It's unlikely that every member will get exactly what they want, so it's important to find a solution that everyone can live with. This may involve making trade-offs, finding creative solutions, or prioritizing different factors.

Finally, it's important to consider the impact of the decision on each member of the family. For example, if a decision involves a significant financial commitment, it's important to consider how it will affect the family's budget and financial stability. If a decision involves a change in routine or schedule, it's important to consider how it will impact each member's daily life.

In conclusion, making decisions as a couple or family requires effective communication, a shared understanding of goals and values, compromise, and consideration of the impact of the decision on each member. By following these principles, families can make decisions that promote harmony, respect, and mutual understanding.

Dealing with Difficult Personal Relationship Decisions

Making personal relationship decisions can be difficult and stressful, especially when the decision involves a difficult or complex situation. Here are some steps you can take to navigate through the decision-making process:

1. Define the problem: The first step is to clearly define the problem. This means identifying the specific issue or conflict that is causing you distress in the relationship. Ask yourself what exactly is bothering you and how it is affecting you.

2. Identify your values: Your values play a critical role in your decision-making process. Identify what matters most to you in your personal relationships. Is it trust, honesty, communication, or something else? Understanding your values will help you make a decision that aligns with your principles and beliefs.

3. Consider your options: Once you have defined the problem and identified your values, it's time to consider your options. Think about what you can do to address the issue or conflict. You may need to have a conversation with the other person, seek support from friends or family, or consider ending the relationship altogether.

4. Weigh the pros and cons: Each option you consider will have its own set of pros and cons. Take the time to carefully evaluate each option and weigh the potential outcomes. Consider the short-term and long-term consequences of each decision.

5. Seek support: Making difficult personal relationship decisions can be overwhelming and emotionally draining. Seek support from trusted friends or family members who can provide a listening ear, offer advice, or simply be there for you during this challenging time.

6. Take action: Once you have carefully evaluated your options and weighed the pros and cons, it's time to take action. Choose the option that aligns with your values and feels right for you, and take the necessary steps to move forward.

Remember, making difficult personal relationship decisions can be challenging, but it's important to prioritize your own well-being and happiness. Trust yourself and your instincts, and don't be afraid to seek help if you need it.

Chapter 7

Decision-Making in the Workplace

Making Decisions as a Leader

Making decisions as a leader is a crucial aspect of effective leadership. As a leader, you are responsible for guiding your team or organization towards success, and this requires making a series of decisions that will impact your team and its outcomes. Here are some key considerations when making decisions as a leader:

1. Gather Information: Before making any decision, it is essential to gather all the relevant information. This includes collecting data, consulting with team members, and seeking expert advice.

2. Analyze the Options: Once you have all the necessary information, it's time to analyze the different options available to you. Consider the pros and cons of each option and how they align with your goals.

3. Make a Plan: After analyzing your options, it's time to make a plan. This should include clear objectives, timelines, and resources needed to achieve your goals.

4. Communicate the Decision: As a leader, it is your responsibility to communicate your decision to your team. Make sure to explain the rationale behind your decision, how it aligns with your team's goals, and what actions are needed to achieve success.

5. Evaluate the Outcomes: Once the decision has been made, it's important to evaluate its outcomes. This will help you determine whether your decision was successful or whether adjustments need to be made.

6. Be Open to Feedback: As a leader, it's important to be open to feedback. Encourage your team members to share their thoughts and opinions about your decisions, and be willing to make changes if necessary.

Overall, making decisions as a leader requires careful consideration, thoughtful analysis, and effective communication. By following these key steps, you can make informed decisions that will lead to success for your team or organization.

Empowering Employees to Make Decisions

Empowering employees to make decisions is a crucial aspect of effective leadership. By giving your employees the authority to make decisions, you can create a more engaged and productive workforce, increase job satisfaction, and foster a culture of innovation. Here are some key considerations when empowering employees to make decisions:

1. Define Boundaries: It is essential to define the boundaries of decision-making authority. This includes outlining the types of decisions that employees can make and the level of autonomy they have. By setting clear boundaries, you can ensure that employees feel confident in their decision-making abilities while also maintaining a level of control over the decision-making process.

2. Provide Training: Empowering employees to make decisions requires providing them with the necessary training and resources. This includes training on decision-making techniques, communication skills, and the company's goals and values. Providing adequate training ensures that employees have the skills and knowledge necessary to make informed decisions.

3. Encourage Collaboration: Collaboration is essential for effective decision-making. Encourage employees to work together to make decisions, share ideas, and provide feedback. Collaboration can lead to more creative and innovative solutions.
4. Recognize and Reward Success: When employees make successful decisions, it's important to recognize and reward their efforts. This can include public recognition, bonuses, or promotions. Recognizing and rewarding success can motivate employees to continue making good decisions.

5. Provide Feedback: Providing feedback is essential for improving decision-making skills. Provide constructive feedback on employee decisions, highlighting areas for improvement and providing guidance on how to make better decisions in the future.

6. Trust Your Employees: Trust is essential for empowering employees to make decisions. Trust that your employees have the skills and knowledge necessary to make good decisions. When employees feel trusted, they are more likely to take ownership of their decisions and feel invested in the success of the company.

   Overall, empowering employees to make decisions requires a culture of trust, collaboration, and continuous learning. By providing the necessary training and resources, recognizing success, and providing feedback, you can create a workforce that is engaged, motivated, and capable of making informed decisions.

Creating a Culture of Smart Decision-Making

Creating a culture of smart decision-making means fostering an environment where individuals and teams are encouraged to make informed, thoughtful, and effective decisions. It involves establishing processes, values, and behaviors that prioritize data-driven and objective decision-making.

Here are some ways to create a culture of smart decision-making:

1. Encourage collaboration: Collaboration is an essential ingredient in making smart decisions. Encourage your team members to work together, share their thoughts and ideas, and provide feedback to one another.

Collaborating with others brings diversity of thought, which can lead to better decision-making.

2. Emphasize data-driven decision-making: Encourage your team to use data to inform their decisions. Ensure that data is readily available and easily accessible. Emphasize the importance of analyzing data, drawing insights, and making decisions based on evidence rather than intuition or personal bias.

3. Foster a growth mindset: Emphasize the importance of continuous learning and growth. Encourage your team to seek out new information, learn from their mistakes, and be open to new perspectives. A growth mindset helps individuals and teams to adapt and make better decisions in changing circumstances.

4. Prioritize clarity and transparency: Ensure that all decisions are made with clarity and transparency. Ensure that everyone involved in the decision-making process understands the objectives, criteria, and consequences of the decision. This promotes accountability and ownership of the decision-making process.

5. Celebrate successes and learn from failures: Celebrate successful decision-making outcomes and recognize the contributions of those involved. Similarly, when decisions lead to negative outcomes, use these experiences as opportunities for learning and growth.

Creating a culture of smart decision-making takes time and effort. However, with the right processes, values, and behaviors in place, it is possible to establish a workplace where effective decision-making is the norm.

Chapter 8

Ethical Decision-Making

Understanding the Ethics of Decision-Making

Understanding the ethics of decision-making means being aware of the moral principles and values that guide decision-making and ensuring that the decisions made are consistent with these principles. Ethical decision-making involves considering the potential consequences of decisions on individuals, society, and the environment, and striving to make decisions that are fair, just, and responsible.

Here are some key factors to consider when it comes to understanding the ethics of decision-making:

1. Recognize the impact of decisions: Every decision has the potential to impact others. It is important to consider the potential consequences of the decision on all stakeholders, including employees, customers, shareholders, and the community.

2. Consider moral principles: Decision-making should be guided by moral principles such as honesty, fairness, responsibility, respect for human dignity, and concern for the well-being of others. These principles can help to ensure that decisions are ethical and that they contribute to the greater good.

3. Be aware of biases: Individuals have biases and prejudices that can influence their decision-making. It is important to recognize these biases and strive to make decisions that are free from personal bias and prejudice.

4. Seek advice and input: Decision-making should not be done in isolation. Seek input and advice from others, including experts and stakeholders, to ensure that decisions are well-informed and consider different perspectives.

5. Hold yourself and others accountable: Ethical decision-making requires accountability. Hold yourself and others accountable for the decisions made, and be prepared to take responsibility for the consequences of those decisions.

In summary, ethical decision-making requires a conscious effort to understand the impact of decisions, consider moral principles, be aware of biases, seek input and advice, and hold oneself and others accountable. By doing so, individuals and organizations can make decisions that are not only effective but also ethical and responsible.

Applying Ethical Frameworks to Your Decisions

Applying ethical frameworks to your decisions means using a structured approach to guide your decision-making process in a morally responsible manner. Ethical frameworks are sets of principles or guidelines that help individuals assess whether an action is morally right or wrong. These frameworks provide a framework for analyzing and evaluating moral dilemmas and making ethical decisions.

There are several ethical frameworks that can be applied to decision-making. Some of the most commonly used frameworks include:

1. Utilitarianism: This framework suggests that the best decision is the one that creates the greatest good for the greatest number of people. When applying this framework, you must weigh the costs and benefits of each alternative and choose the one that maximizes overall happiness or utility.

2. Deontology: This framework emphasizes the importance of following moral rules or duties. According to this framework, some actions are intrinsically right or wrong, regardless of their consequences. When applying this framework, you must consider whether an action violates a moral rule or duty, such as telling the truth or respecting human dignity.

3. Virtue Ethics: This framework emphasizes the importance of cultivating virtues or moral character traits, such as honesty, kindness, and courage. According to this framework, the best decision is the one that reflects a virtuous character. When applying this framework, you must consider how your decision reflects your own character and the character of others involved in the situation.

4. Care Ethics: This framework emphasizes the importance of relationships and caring for others. According to this framework, the best decision is the one that promotes caring and compassion for others. When applying this framework, you must consider how your decision affects those who are vulnerable or dependent on others.

When applying ethical frameworks to your decisions, it is important to consider the specific context of the situation, the values of those involved, and the potential consequences of each decision.

Dealing with Ethical Dilemmas in decision

Ethical dilemmas can arise when decision-makers are faced with situations in which there are conflicting moral values or principles. The process of dealing with ethical dilemmas in decision-making requires careful consideration and analysis of the competing values and principles involved. Here are some steps that can help in dealing with ethical dilemmas:

1. Identify the ethical dilemma: The first step in dealing with an ethical dilemma is to identify it. This involves recognizing that there is a conflict between two or more moral values or principles.

2. Gather information: Once the ethical dilemma has been identified, it is important to gather as much information as possible about the situation. This includes gathering information about the people involved, the context in which the situation has arisen, and any relevant laws or policies.

3. Identify the stakeholders: In any ethical dilemma, there are likely to be stakeholders who are affected by the decision. It is important to identify these stakeholders and consider their interests and needs.

4. Consider the options: After gathering all the relevant information and identifying the stakeholders, it is important to consider the available options for resolving the ethical dilemma. This may involve weighing the pros and cons of each option and considering the impact on the stakeholders.

5. Apply ethical principles: Once the options have been considered, it is important to apply ethical principles to the decision-making process. This may involve using principles such as autonomy, beneficence, non-maleficence, and justice to guide the decision-making process.

6. Make a decision: After weighing all the options and considering the ethical principles involved, a decision should be made. This decision should be based on the best interests of the stakeholders and should be consistent with ethical principles.

7. Reflect on the decision: Once a decision has been made, it is important to reflect on the decision-making process and the outcome. This reflection can help to identify any areas for improvement and can inform future decision-making processes.

Dealing with ethical dilemmas in decision-making can be challenging, but by following these steps, decision-makers can ensure that they are making decisions that are consistent with ethical principles and in the best interests of all stakeholders involved.

Chapter 9

Long-Term Decision-Making

The Importance of Thinking Ahead

Thinking ahead refers to the process of anticipating future events, opportunities, and challenges and making plans to address them. It is an important skill that helps individuals and organizations prepare for the future and make better decisions. Here are some reasons why thinking ahead is important:

1. Anticipating future challenges: Thinking ahead allows individuals and organizations to anticipate future challenges and prepare for them. By identifying potential obstacles and developing plans to address them, individuals and organizations can minimize the impact of these challenges and reduce the likelihood of failure.

2. Identifying future opportunities: Thinking ahead also allows individuals and organizations to identify future opportunities and capitalize on them. By recognizing trends and changes in the market or industry, individuals and organizations can position themselves to take advantage of these opportunities and gain a competitive advantage.

3. Making better decisions: When individuals and organizations think ahead, they can make better decisions. By considering the potential consequences of different options and weighing the pros and cons, individuals and organizations can make informed decisions that are more likely to lead to positive outcomes.

4. Creating a sense of purpose: Thinking ahead can also create a sense of purpose and direction. By setting goals and developing plans to achieve them, individuals and organizations can have a clear vision of what they want to accomplish and how they plan to get there.

5. Improving efficiency: When individuals and organizations think ahead, they can improve efficiency by eliminating waste and unnecessary steps. By anticipating future needs and planning accordingly, individuals and organizations can streamline their processes and reduce costs.

Overall, thinking ahead is an important skill that can help individuals and organizations to prepare for the future, make better decisions, and achieve their goals. By taking the time to anticipate future events and develop plans to address them, individuals and organizations can stay ahead of the curve and succeed in a constantly changing world.

Making Decisions That Serve Your Long-Term Goals

Making decisions that serve your long-term goals is an important skill that can help you achieve success in all areas of your life. By considering your long-term goals and making decisions that align with them, you can stay focused, make progress, and achieve the outcomes you desire. Here are some strategies that can help you make decisions that serve your long-term goals:

1. Identify your long-term goals: The first step in making decisions that serve your long-term goals is to identify what those goals are. This may involve reflecting on your values, passions, and aspirations, and setting specific, measurable, and achievable goals that align with them.

2. Prioritize your goals: Once you have identified your long-term goals, it is important to prioritize them. This may involve considering which goals are most important to you, which ones will have the greatest impact on your life, and which ones are most achievable given your current circumstances.

3. Consider the potential outcomes: When making decisions, it is important to consider the potential outcomes and how they will impact your long-term goals. This may involve weighing the pros and cons of different options and considering the potential risks and rewards of each.

4. Evaluate the impact on your long-term goals: Before making a decision, it is important to evaluate the impact that it will have on your long-term goals. This may involve considering how the decision will help you move closer to your goals or how it may hinder your progress.

5. Take action: Once you have evaluated the potential outcomes and impact on your long-term goals, it is time to take action. This may involve making a

decision, taking a specific course of action, or implementing a plan to achieve your long-term goals.

6. Monitor your progress: Finally, it is important to monitor your progress and adjust your actions as needed. This may involve tracking your progress towards your long-term goals, evaluating the effectiveness of your decisions, and making adjustments as needed to stay on track.

By following these strategies, you can make decisions that serve your long-term goals and achieve success in all areas of your life. By staying focused on your goals and making decisions that align with them, you can stay motivated, make progress, and achieve the outcomes you desire.

Avoiding Short-Term Thinking and Impulsive Decisions

Avoiding short-term thinking and impulsive decisions is crucial for long-term success and personal growth. Short-term thinking and impulsive decisions can lead to a range of negative consequences, including missed opportunities, decreased productivity, and long-term setbacks. Here are some strategies that can help you avoid short-term thinking and impulsive decisions:

1. Develop a long-term perspective: One of the most important ways to avoid short-term thinking and impulsive decisions is to develop a long-term perspective. This means looking beyond immediate gratification and considering how your actions will impact your future goals and aspirations.

2. Set clear goals: Setting clear goals is another important strategy for avoiding short-term thinking and impulsive decisions. By setting specific, measurable, and achievable goals, you can stay focused on what you want to achieve and avoid distractions and temptations that may lead to impulsive decisions.

3. Consider the consequences: Before making a decision, it is important to consider the potential consequences. This means evaluating how your

decision will impact your long-term goals, as well as considering the short-term risks and rewards.

4. Seek advice and feedback: Seeking advice and feedback from others can also help you avoid short-term thinking and impulsive decisions. This may involve consulting with a mentor or trusted friend, or seeking the advice of a professional who can offer an objective perspective.

5. Take time to reflect: Taking time to reflect on your goals, values, and priorities can also help you avoid short-term thinking and impulsive decisions. This may involve setting aside time each day to reflect on your progress, or taking regular breaks to clear your mind and refocus your energy.

6. Practice self-control: Finally, practicing self-control is essential for avoiding short-term thinking and impulsive decisions. This means learning to resist temptation, delaying gratification, and staying focused on your long-term goals and aspirations.

By following these strategies, you can avoid short-term thinking and impulsive decisions and achieve long-term success and personal growth.

By developing a long-term perspective, setting clear goals, considering the consequences, seeking advice and feedback, taking time to reflect, and practicing self-control, you can stay focused on what matters most and make decisions that align with your values and aspirations.

Chapter 10

Decision-Making for Success

Applying Decision-Making to Achieve Success

Effective decision-making is a critical skill for achieving success in all areas of life. Whether you are trying to grow your career, build a business, or achieve personal goals, the ability to make effective decisions can help you stay focused, motivated, and productive. Here are some strategies for applying decision-making to achieve success:

1. Define your goals: The first step in applying decision-making to achieve success is to define your goals. This means identifying what you want to achieve and setting clear, specific, and measurable goals that align with your values and aspirations.

2. Gather information: Once you have defined your goals, it is important to gather information that can help you make informed decisions. This may involve researching different options, talking to experts, and gathering data and feedback from others.

3. Evaluate options: With information in hand, it is time to evaluate your options. This means considering the pros and cons of different alternatives, assessing their potential risks and rewards, and weighing how each option aligns with your goals and values.

4. Make a decision: After evaluating your options, it is time to make a decision. This may involve choosing a specific course of action, selecting a partner or team, or making a commitment to a specific goal or outcome.

5. Take action: Once you have made a decision, it is time to take action. This means putting your plan into motion, staying focused on your goals, and taking concrete steps to achieve success.

6. Monitor progress: Finally, it is important to monitor your progress and evaluate the effectiveness of your decisions. This may involve tracking your progress towards your goals, assessing the impact of your decisions, and making adjustments as needed to stay on track.

By applying decision-making to achieve success, you can stay focused, motivated, and productive, even in the face of challenges and setbacks.

 By defining your goals, gathering information, evaluating options, making decisions, taking action, and monitoring progress, you can achieve your goals, build your skills, and grow your career or business. Ultimately, effective decision-making is a powerful tool that can help you achieve success in all areas of your life.

Developing Good Decision-Making Habits

Developing good decision-making habits is essential for success in both personal and professional life. Making sound decisions is not just about considering the available options and choosing the best one, but it also involves a set of habits and skills that need to be developed over time. Here are some ways to develop good decision-making habits:

1. Define your objectives: Before making any decision, it is essential to know what you want to achieve. Clarify your objectives and ensure that the decision you make is in line with your goals.

2. Gather information: Gather as much information as possible about the options available to you. The more information you have, the better-informed your decision will be.

3. Evaluate your options: Consider the pros and cons of each option and evaluate them based on how they align with your objectives.

4. Consider the consequences: Think about the potential consequences of each option. Consider the impact of your decision on yourself, others, and the environment.

5. Consult with others: Seek the opinions of others, especially those who have experience in the area you are making a decision about. However, ultimately, the decision is yours to make.

6. Take your time: Do not rush into making a decision. Take the time to think through the options available to you and the potential consequences of each one.

7. Trust your gut: After you have gathered all the necessary information, analyzed your options, and considered the consequences, trust your instincts. Sometimes, your intuition can be a powerful guide.

8. Learn from your mistakes: No one makes perfect decisions all the time. It is essential to learn from your mistakes and use them as opportunities for growth and improvement.

   In conclusion, developing good decision-making habits is a skill that takes time, practice, and patience to master. By following these tips, you can improve your decision-making abilities and make better choices in both your personal and professional life.

Avoiding Decision-Making Traps

Decision-making is an essential skill that individuals and organizations need to master to achieve their objectives. However, decision-making is not always easy, and individuals may fall into decision-making traps that can negatively impact the quality of their decisions. These traps are biases or errors in thinking that lead to faulty decision-making.

To avoid decision-making traps, it is important to understand their nature and how they manifest in decision-making processes. Some common decision-making traps include:

1. Confirmation bias: This is the tendency to seek out information that confirms our pre-existing beliefs and to ignore or discount information that contradicts our beliefs. To avoid this trap, individuals should actively seek out diverse perspectives and challenge their assumptions.

2. Anchoring bias: This is the tendency to rely too heavily on the first piece of information encountered when making a decision, even if it is irrelevant. To avoid this trap, individuals should consider a range of information sources and avoid relying too heavily on a single piece of information.

3. Sunk cost fallacy: This is the tendency to continue investing in a project or decision based on the resources already invested, even if the decision is no longer rational. To avoid this trap, individuals should focus on the future costs and benefits of a decision, rather than the past.

4. Groupthink: This is the tendency of a group to prioritize consensus over individual opinions, leading to conformity and a lack of critical thinking. To avoid this trap, individuals should encourage diverse perspectives and dissenting opinions within a group.

5. Availability bias: This is the tendency to rely on easily available or memorable information when making a decision, rather than seeking out more comprehensive information. To avoid this trap, individuals should actively seek out and consider a wide range of information sources.

To avoid decision-making traps, individuals should be aware of their biases and actively work to challenge them. This can include seeking out diverse perspectives, considering a range of information sources, and encouraging dissenting opinions within groups. Additionally, individuals should engage in critical thinking and reflection, taking the time to consider all options and potential outcomes before making a decision. By doing so, individuals can improve the quality of their decision-making and avoid common decision-making traps.

Chapter 11

Learning from Your Decisions

Evaluating Your Decisions and Learning from Mistakes

Evaluating your decisions and learning from mistakes is an essential skill in decision-making. It involves reflecting on the choices you've made, considering the outcomes, and identifying areas where you could have made a better decision. By doing so, you can learn from your mistakes and make more informed decisions in the future.

Here are some steps you can take to evaluate your decisions and learn from your mistakes:

1. Review the decision-making process: Start by reviewing the decision-making process. Identify the steps you took, the information you considered, and the factors that influenced your decision. This step helps you identify where you might have gone wrong and how to avoid similar mistakes in the future.

2. Evaluate the outcomes: Next, evaluate the outcomes of your decision. Did it achieve the intended result? If not, what went wrong, and what could you have done differently to achieve a better outcome? This step helps you identify areas for improvement and helps you adjust your decision-making process accordingly.

3. Consider alternatives: Consider alternative options and evaluate the outcomes that could have resulted from those decisions. This step helps you identify missed opportunities and helps you broaden your perspective when considering future decisions.

4. Reflect on your emotions and biases: Reflect on your emotions and biases that may have influenced your decision. Consider how they may have impacted your thinking and decision-making process. This step helps you become more aware of your own biases and helps you make more objective decisions in the future.

5. Take action: Finally, take action based on what you've learned. Adjust your decision-making process and implement changes to improve your

decision-making skills. This step helps you apply what you've learned to future decisions and helps you avoid making the same mistakes again.

In summary, evaluating your decisions and learning from mistakes involves reviewing the decision-making process, evaluating outcomes, considering alternatives, reflecting on emotions and biases, and taking action. By doing so, you can make more informed decisions and avoid making the same mistakes in the future.

Building on Your Decision-Making Skills

Building on your decision-making skills is an ongoing process that involves continuously improving and refining your decision-making abilities. Strong decision-making skills are essential for success in both personal and professional settings, and there are several steps you can take to enhance your skills in this area.

Here are some ways you can build on your decision-making skills:

1. Identify your strengths and weaknesses: Start by identifying your strengths and weaknesses in decision-making. This can help you understand your areas of expertise and where you may need to focus your efforts on improving. You may want to seek feedback from others to get a more objective view of your decision-making abilities.

2. Seek out new experiences: One of the best ways to improve your decision-making skills is to seek out new experiences. This could involve trying new activities, taking on new responsibilities, or challenging yourself in different ways. By exposing yourself to new situations, you can develop your ability to make sound decisions under a variety of circumstances.

3. Learn from others: Learning from others is another effective way to build on your decision-making skills. Seek out mentors, coaches, or colleagues who have strong decision-making abilities and ask them for advice or guidance. You can also study case studies of successful decision-makers or attend workshops or training sessions on decision-making.

4. Practice decision-making: Like any skill, decision-making requires practice. Take advantage of opportunities to make decisions and practice your decision-making abilities. This could involve making decisions in your personal life or seeking out opportunities to make decisions in your professional life.

5. Reflect on your decisions: Finally, it's essential to reflect on your decisions and evaluate the outcomes. This can help you identify areas for improvement and refine your decision-making process over time.

In summary, building on your decision-making skills involves identifying your strengths and weaknesses, seeking out new experiences, learning from others, practicing decision-making, and reflecting on your decisions. By continuously improving your decision-making abilities, you can enhance your overall effectiveness and achieve greater success in your personal and professional life.

The Importance of Reflection and Continuous Improvement

Reflection and continuous improvement are critical components of effective decision making, as they enable individuals and organizations to learn from past experiences, evaluate their performance, and make necessary adjustments to improve future outcomes. In essence, reflection involves taking the time to review and analyze past decisions, experiences, and outcomes, while continuous improvement involves using that information to make changes and improve future performance.

One of the key benefits of reflection and continuous improvement is that they enable individuals and organizations to identify and address areas of weakness and to capitalize on areas of strength. By reflecting on past decisions and outcomes, individuals can identify the factors that contributed to success or failure, and use that information to make more informed decisions in the future. Similarly, by engaging in continuous improvement, individuals and organizations can identify ways to improve processes, procedures, and systems, leading to increased efficiency, effectiveness, and productivity.

Another important benefit of reflection and continuous improvement is that they promote self-awareness and self-reflection, which are critical components of personal and professional development. By reflecting on their decisions and experiences, individuals can gain a better understanding of their own strengths and weaknesses, identify areas for growth and development, and ultimately become more effective decision makers.

Moreover, reflection and continuous improvement are essential for organizations that want to remain competitive and adapt to changing market conditions. By continuously evaluating and improving their processes and systems, organizations can respond more quickly to changes in the marketplace, stay ahead of the competition, and achieve long-term success.

In conclusion, reflection and continuous improvement are essential components of effective decision making. By taking the time to reflect on past experiences, evaluate performance, and make necessary improvements, individuals and organizations can identify areas for growth, capitalize on areas of strength, and ultimately make better decisions and achieve greater success.

Chapter 12

Making the Best Decision: Putting It All Together

Applying the Principles of Smart Decision-Making

Smart decision-making is a process that involves weighing different options and selecting the best course of action based on a set of guiding principles. There are several key principles that can help individuals and organizations make smart decisions, including the following:

1. Clearly Define the Problem: One of the first steps in smart decision-making is clearly defining the problem or issue at hand. This involves identifying the goals, constraints, and other factors that are relevant to the decision. Without a clear understanding of the problem, it is difficult to make an informed decision.

2. Gather and Analyze Information: Once the problem is clearly defined, it is important to gather and analyze information related to the decision. This may involve researching the options available, consulting with experts, and analyzing data to identify trends and patterns.

3. Identify and Evaluate Options: After gathering and analyzing information, it is time to identify and evaluate the available options. This involves considering the pros and cons of each option, and weighing the potential risks and benefits of each.

4. Consider the Consequences: Before making a final decision, it is important to consider the potential consequences of each option. This may involve assessing the short-term and long-term effects of each option, as well as considering how the decision may impact other areas of the organization or individual's life.

5. Make a Decision: Once all of the relevant information has been gathered and evaluated, it is time to make a decision. This involves selecting the option that is most likely to achieve the desired outcome, based on the principles of rationality, fairness, and efficiency.

6. Implement the Decision: After making a decision, it is important to implement the chosen course of action. This involves putting the decision

into action, monitoring the results, and making any necessary adjustments along the way.

7. Learn from the Outcome: Finally, it is important to reflect on the outcome of the decision and learn from the experience. This involves evaluating the results of the decision, identifying areas for improvement, and using that information to make better decisions in the future.

By applying these principles of smart decision-making, individuals and organizations can make informed decisions that are more likely to achieve the desired outcome. The process is iterative and ongoing, and requires a willingness to gather and analyze information, consider multiple options, and learn from past experiences.

Integrating Decision-Making into Your Life

Integrating decision-making into your life involves developing a deliberate and intentional approach to making choices that align with your goals and values. It requires taking a proactive role in shaping your life rather than simply reacting to circumstances or following the path of least resistance.

Here are some steps you can take to integrate decision-making into your life:

1. Define your values and goals: Before you can make decisions that align with your values and goals, you need to know what they are. Take time to reflect on what is important to you, what motivates you, and what you want to achieve in your life.
2. Consider your options: Once you have a clear understanding of your values and goals, think about the different options available to you. Consider the pros and cons of each option and how each choice would impact your life in the short and long term.
3. Gather information: Make informed decisions by gathering information from a variety of sources. Research your options, talk to people who have

experience in the areas you are considering, and seek advice from trusted advisors.

4. Evaluate your decision-making process: After you make a decision, evaluate your process to see if it was effective. Did you consider all relevant information? Did you weigh the pros and cons of each option? Were you true to your values and goals?

5. Be open to change: Finally, remember that decision-making is an ongoing process, and it's okay to change your mind if new information comes to light or if your goals and values shift over time.

Integrating decision-making into your life requires a commitment to being intentional and proactive in shaping your life. By following these steps, you can make choices that align with your values and goals and move you closer to the life you want to live.

Making the Best Decision at All Times

Making the best decision at all times can be challenging, as there are often multiple factors to consider and various potential outcomes to weigh. However, there are several strategies you can use to improve your decision-making and increase the likelihood of making the best choice in any situation.

1. Define the problem: Before you can make the best decision, you need to define the problem or issue you are trying to solve. Take the time to clearly understand the situation, identify the root cause of the problem, and define the desired outcome.

2. Gather information: Once you have defined the problem, gather as much information as possible to help you make an informed decision. This may involve conducting research, seeking advice from experts, and talking to people who have experience with similar situations.

3. Evaluate your options: After gathering information, evaluate your options and weigh the pros and cons of each. Consider the potential outcomes of each option and how they align with your values, goals, and priorities.

4. Consider the long-term impact: When making decisions, it's essential to consider the long-term impact of your choices. Ask yourself how each option will affect you and others in the future, and consider whether the short-term benefits are worth any potential long-term consequences.

5. Seek input from others: Sometimes, it can be helpful to get input from others when making a decision. This may involve seeking advice from friends or family members, consulting with a mentor or coach, or seeking feedback from colleagues or experts in the field.

6. Trust your instincts: While it's essential to gather information and consider various options, it's also important to trust your instincts and intuition. If something feels off or doesn't align with your values, listen to that feeling and consider it when making your decision.

7. Be open to change: Finally, remember that decision-making is an ongoing process, and it's okay to change your mind if new information comes to light or if your circumstances change.

By following these strategies, you can improve your decision-making and increase the likelihood of making the best choice in any situation. However, it's important to remember that no decision is perfect, and there may be unforeseen consequences no matter what option you choose. Focus on making the best decision you can with the information you have at the time, and be prepared to adjust your course if necessary.

Conclusion

Recap of Key Takeaways in decision making

Recapping key takeaways is an essential part of decision-making processes, as it helps to ensure that all participants are on the same page and have a clear understanding of the relevant facts, opinions, and options. By summarizing the most important points and highlighting key themes or trends, decision-makers can more effectively weigh the pros and cons of different courses of action and make informed choices.

There are several ways that recapping key takeaways can be particularly useful in decision-making processes. For example:

1. Encourages critical thinking: When participants are asked to recap key takeaways, they are forced to think critically about the information that has been presented and evaluate it in terms of its relevance and importance.
2. Provides a shared understanding: Recapping key takeaways helps to ensure that everyone involved in the decision-making process has a shared understanding of the situation at hand, including the relevant factors, opinions, and options.
3. Helps to identify gaps or inconsistencies: By summarizing the key takeaways, decision-makers can identify any gaps or inconsistencies in the information presented, which can help to inform further research or discussion.
4. Enables effective communication: Recapping key takeaways can also facilitate effective communication between participants, as it helps to ensure that everyone is speaking the same language and has a clear understanding of the issues at hand.

Overall, recapping key takeaways is an important tool for decision-makers, as it helps to ensure that they have all of the information they need to make informed choices and achieve their desired outcomes. By summarizing the most important points and identifying key themes or trends, decision-makers can more effectively weigh the pros and cons of different options and choose the best course of action for their specific situation.

Final Thoughts and Encouragement

Making decisions can be a challenging process, especially when there are multiple factors to consider and potential outcomes to evaluate. However, it's important to remember that every decision we make can ultimately shape our lives and lead us towards our goals and aspirations.

To make effective decisions, it's essential to gather as much information as possible and evaluate all possible outcomes. This may involve researching various options, seeking advice from trusted sources, and weighing the pros and cons of each potential choice.

It's also important to trust your intuition and listen to your inner voice when making decisions. While it's crucial to consider the advice and opinions of others, ultimately, you are the only one who knows what is best for you.

Remember that making a decision is better than not making one at all. Procrastination and indecisiveness can lead to missed opportunities and a lack of progress. Even if a decision doesn't turn out as planned, it can provide valuable learning experiences and lead to new opportunities.

In conclusion, decision-making can be a challenging process, but it's essential to trust yourself, gather information, and evaluate all possible outcomes. Every decision has the potential to shape your life, so it's important to take the time to make well-informed and thoughtful choices.